THE TRAGEDY
OF TODAY'S GAYS

I LOVE BEING GAY. I LOVE GAY PEOPLE. I THINK WE'RE BETTER THAN OTHER PEOPLE. I REALLY DO. I THINK WE'RE SMARTER AND MORE TALENTED AND MORE AWARE. I DO, I DO, I TOTALLY DO. I REALLY DO THINK ALL OF THESE THINGS. AND I TRY VERY HARD TO REMEMBER ALL THIS. I LOVE BEING GAY. I LOVE GAY PEOPLE. I THINK WE'RE BETTER THAN OTHER PEOPLE. I REALLY DO. I THINK WE'RE SMARTER AND MORE TALENTED AND MORE AWARE. I DO, I DO, I TOTALLY DO. I REALLY DO THINK ALL OF THESE THINGS. AND I TRY VERY HARD TO REMEMBER ALL THIS. I LOVE BEING GAY. I LOVE GAY PEOPLE. I THINK WE'RE BETTER THAN OTHER PEOPLE. I REALLY DO. I THINK WE'RE SMARTER AND MORE TALENTED AND MORE AWARE. I DO, I DO, I TOTALLY DO. I REALLY DO THINK ALL OF THESE THINGS. AND I TRY VERY HARD TO REMEMBER ALL THIS. I LOVE BEING GAY. I LOVE GAY PEOPLE. I THINK WE'RE BETTER THAN OTHER PEOPLE. I REALLY DO. I THINK WE'RE SMARTER AND MORE TALENTED AND MORE AWARE. I DO, I DO, I TOTALLY DO. I REALLY DO THINK ALL OF THESE THINGS. AND I TRY VERY HARD TO REMEMBER ALL THIS. I LOVE BEING GAY. I LOVE GAY PEOPLE. I THINK WE'RE BETTER THAN OTHER PEOPLE. I REALLY DO. I THINK WE'RE SMARTER AND MORE TALENTED AND MORE AWARE. I DO, I DO, I TOTALLY DO. I REALLY DO THINK ALL OF THESE THINGS. AND I TRY VERY HARD TO REMEMBER ALL THIS. I LOVE BEING GAY. I LOVE GAY PEOPLE. I THINK WE'RE BETTER THAN OTHER PEOPLE. I REALLY DO. I THINK WE'RE SMARTER AND MORE TALENTED AND MORE AWARE. I DO, I DO, I TOTALLY DO. I REALLY DO THINK ALL OF THESE THINGS. AND I TRY VERY HARD TO REMEMBER ALL THIS. I LOVE BEING GAY. I LOVE GAY PEOPLE. I THINK WE'RE BETTER THAN OTHER PEOPLE. I REALLY DO. I THINK WE'RE SMARTER AND MORE TALENTED AND MORE AWARE. I DO, I DO, I TOTALLY DO. I REALLY DO THINK ALL OF THESE THINGS. AND I TRY VERY HARD TO REMEMBER ALL THIS.

I LOVE BEING GAY. I LOVE GAY PEOPLE. I THINK WE'RE BETTER THAN OTHER PEOPLE. I REALLY DO. I THINK WE'RE SMARTER AND MORE TALENTED AND MORE AWARE. I DO, I DO, I TOTALLY DO. I REALLY DO THINK ALL OF THESE THINGS. AND I TRY VERY HARD TO REMEMBER ALL THIS.

I LOVE BEING GAY. I LOVE GAY PEOPLE. I THINK WE'RE BETTER THAN OTHER PEOPLE. I REALLY DO. I THINK WE'RE SMARTER AND MORE TALENTED AND MORE AWARE. I DO, I DO, I TOTALLY DO. I REALLY DO THINK ALL OF THESE THINGS. AND I TRY VERY HARD TO REMEMBER ALL THIS. I LOVE BEING GAY. I LOVE GAY PEOPLE. I THINK WE'RE BETTER THAN OTHER PEOPLE. I REALLY DO. I THINK WE'RE SMARTER AND MORE TALENTED AND MORE AWARE. I DO, I DO, I TOTALLY DO. I REALLY DO THINK ALL OF THESE THINGS. AND I TRY VERY HARD TO REMEMBER ALL THIS. I LOVE BEING GAY. I LOVE GAY PEOPLE. I THINK WE'RE BETTER THAN OTHER PEOPLE. I REALLY DO. I THINK WE'RE SMARTER AND MORE TALENTED AND MORE AWARE. I DO, I DO, I TOTALLY DO. I REALLY DO THINK ALL OF THESE THINGS. AND I TRY VERY HARD TO REMEMBER ALL THIS.

THE TRAGEDY
OF TODAY'S GAYS

LARRY KRAMER

JEREMY P. TARCHER/PENGUIN
A MEMBER OF PENGUIN GROUP (USA) INC.
NEW YORK

JEREMY P. TARCHER/PENGUIN
Published by the Penguin Group
Penguin Group (USA) Inc. 375 Hudson Street, New York, New York
10014, USA • Penguin Group (Canada), 10 Alcorn Avenue, Toronto, Ontario
M4V 3B2, Canada (a division of Pearson Penguin Canada Inc.) • Penguin Books
Ltd, 80 Strand, London WC2R 0RL, England • Penguin Ireland, 25 St Stephen's
Green, Dublin 2, Ireland (a division of Penguin Books Ltd) • Penguin Group
(Australia), 250 Camberwell Road, Camberwell, Victoria 3124, Australia (a
division of Pearson Australia Group Pty Ltd) • Penguin Books India Pvt Ltd, 11
Community Centre, Panchsheel Park, New Delhi–110 017, India • Penguin
Group (NZ), Cnr Airborne and Rosedale Roads, Albany, Auckland 1310, New
Zealand (a division of Pearson New Zealand Ltd) • Penguin Books (South Africa)
(Pty) Ltd, 24 Sturdee Avenue, Rosebank, Johannesburg 2196, South Africa

Penguin Books Ltd, Registered Offices:
80 Strand, London WC2R 0RL, England

Most Tarcher/Penguin books are available at special quantity discounts for bulk
purchase for sales promotions, premiums, fund-raising, and educational needs.
Special books or book excerpts also can be created to fit specific needs. For
details, write Penguin Group (USA) Inc. Special Markets, 375 Hudson Street,
New York, NY 10014.

Library of Congress Cataloging-in-Publication Data

Kramer, Larry.
    The tragedy of today's gays / Larry Kramer.
      p.   cm.
    ISBN 1-58542-427-7
    1. Gays—United States—Social conditions.   2. Gay men—United States—
Social conditions.   3. Gays—Government policy—United States.
4. Homophobia—United States.   5. AIDS (Disease)—Social aspects.   I. Title.
HQ76.3.U5K73   2005   2005041742
306.76'62—dc22

Printed in the United States of America
10 9 8 7 6 5 4 3 2 1

This book is printed on acid-free paper. ♾

Book design by Stephanie Huntwork

For Will Schwalbe

Four score and seven years ago our fathers brought forth on this continent a new nation, conceived in liberty and dedicated to the proposition that all men are created equal.

—*Abraham Lincoln*

ACKNOWLEDGMENTS

I would like to acknowledge the help of Rodger McFarlane, Will Schwalbe, and my partner, David Webster, in preparing this book. I am grateful to Rodger and Linda Bush at the Gill Foundation for educating me about Lewis Powell and the Powell Manifesto, about which I had been previously ignorant. Thanks to Bill Moyers and his producer, Peter Meryash, for the use of his extraordinary speech, which is quoted here.

I am grateful to Daniel Carlson and his HIV Forum, which mounted my speech, "The Tragedy of Today's Gays," with help from New York University's Office of Lesbian, Gay, Bisexual, and Transgendered Student Services, Broadway Cares/Equity Fights AIDS, the Callen-Lorde Community Health Center, and the Gill Foundation. Dan was indefatigable in getting me going and then getting the word out so that Cooper Union was full. Tom Viola of BC/EFA has been a devoted supporter of my work for many years; he has always been there for me in whatever I have wanted to do and say. There have not been many like him in my life. Peter Staley, Jeff Witty, and Michael Brown all helped to get me off my ass.

Ken Siman of Tarcher/Penguin has proved to be an editor of consummate and impressive skill, perseverance, and patience. I have been blessed with exceptional editors at each of my publishers; I am happy to add Ken to that short list.

I thank Naomi Wolf and Rodger for their contributions to this volume. They should know that I never believe anything good that is said about me.

I offer a special additional thank-you to Will Schwalbe. I like to say that I have known Will since before he was born, since his amazing mother, Mary Anne, is one of my oldest and most precious friends. I have watched him grow into the most amazing person, a proud gay man of incredible wisdom and skill. Although he is editor in chief of Hyperion books, he also participates in a great deal of my life. He is the editor of my book *The American People,* he is on the board of the Larry Kramer Initiative for Lesbian and Gay Studies at Yale, he is my literary executor as well as one of the executors of my estate, and he is quite possibly the only person in the world who can get me to do something when I have dug my heels in otherwise. I guess that means that I could not get along without him. This is true.

Thanks to them all. I am proud of this book, and it would not be here without them.

CONTENTS

FOREWORD
BY NAOMI WOLF

OF COURSE, I HAD HEARD OF *FAGGOTS*, growing up as I did in San Francisco in the 1970s; it seemed that everyone in town, for a time, gay and straight, was reading it. But preoccupied with my teenaged concerns, I did not seek it out.

It was not until I was a young adult—and trying to be a writer myself—that I encountered Larry Kramer's work myself for the first time. I was taken by a gay friend to a production of *The Normal Heart*. It was New York at the beginning of what became known as "the plague years." The world of sexuality was darkening. The Reagan administration had allowed our collective understanding of the AIDS crisis to fall into the lines of a moral indictment. The right, it seemed, had skillfully, even artistically, claimed a moral frame for the suffering that gay men—and later IV drug users—were undergoing.

I did not expect *The Normal Heart* to speak directly to me, a straight woman. To my astonishment, I sat, riveted—more than riveted: called to; challenged as if by a higher self—for the duration of the play. Ned Weeks's confrontation with the plague that was starting to take prisoners among his friends—his confrontation with his own responsibility to speak and to act—was not a "gay" journey but a universal one. Kramer had used his gifts as a writer—gifts of wit, because he is funny; of characterization, because he is acutely observant; and of pathos, because he has a great heart—to make Weeks's anguish my own. The struggle to face himself that Ned Weeks, Kramer's alter ego here as well as in *The Destiny of Me,* undergoes transcended "identity politics" or activism or even the historical moment to which it spoke so clearly and compellingly. Weeks's journey, because of Kramer's in some ways old-fashioned skill as a writer, became archetypal.

That evening changed my own life. I had entered the theater uncertain how "we"—that is, those of us who longed for an America more inclusive and just than the one being constructed by the religious and economic right—could ever re-claim the language and consciousness of morality. I left the theater knowing what that language would sound like. No one else on the left at that time—with the rare exception of some activists trained in the black church, and some progressive religious leaders—ever used the moral framework that is so much a part of Kramer's voice, and that the right had coopted so skillfully. Conscience, responsibility, calling; truth and lies, clarity of purpose or abandonment of one's moral calling; loyalty and be-trayal—these terms framed Ned Weeks's emerging consciousness, in this play and in the later *The Destiny of Me.* In my stagestruck ardor, I fired off the only fan letter I have ever written—thanking Larry Kramer for showing me how a contemporary writer can have a moral vision and use words to make change in the real world.

As I mentioned, Larry Kramer has a great heart; he wrote kindly back to the awestruck twentysomething who had never published.

Since that first encounter with the possibilities

that his language opened up in my mind, I followed Kramer's work closely. I watched the famous activism of the 1980s and 1990s; the man reviled for his prophetic warnings to his own community about AIDS; a founder of both Gay Men's Health Crisis and the activist organization ACT UP; the gadfly to the medical establishment; and, more belatedly, the lionized éminence grise. As *The Destiny of Me* was wreathed with honors; as *Faggots* went into printing after printing; as his collected essays emerged; as *The Normal Heart* was revived, to great acclaim, at a twentieth-anniversary celebration—I continued to wonder, in some ways, about the role of Kramer's reputation; not about the acclaim and the hostility—those were perfectly explainable, and Kramer himself has been eloquent, in his speeches and essays—including this one—explaining them.

No—what I wondered about was why Kramer's tremendous power as a literary gadfly—as a polemicist, an activist with his words—seemed to overshadow the deeper accomplishment that I saw in his writing. To me, Kramer is a great writer of our generation not primarily because of his polemic or his activism. He is a great writer because of how he uses his humanism in his work.

"Humanism" is a vexed and old-fashioned word, now out of favor. Yet Kramer is, I argue, a great humanist writer in the humanist tradition. I mean by that that what makes his work resonate is precisely the way he demands to include the crisis of contemporary gay life in the accounting of the human experience. He is radical *not* because he is playing identity politics—he doesn't—but because he insists that *this* voiceless or homeless gay man, too, is part of the human family, and we must feel what he feels—that *this* crystal meth addict has the same moral challenge, the same confrontation with the great human task of doing right, that the president has. A "humanist" is someone who believes that the creative work of every single individual is profoundly important—a message that underlies his anguished words here. It is an old-fashioned, humanist position to look at many tens of thousands of partying, drug-using young people and grieve not just the loss of their health—a material equation—but the loss of their potential, the cutting short of their human journeys of moral choice, of particular love. Even his play's title reflects his humanism: it's "true of the normal heart" writes W. H. Auden, that "the error bred in the bone / Of each woman and each man / Craves what it cannot have, Not universal love / But to be loved alone." Identity politics, political correctness, even activism, offer "universal love"; Kramer's great achievement is to offer each member of his audience, each of his characters, even himself as he appears, vulnerable and scathingly honest, as a character in the drama of the contemporary scene—the humanist promise of being "loved alone."

This humanism lights up even a satire like *Faggots,* in retrospect. Looking at the graphic sex in the Pines—surveying the action in the Everhard Baths—the book's narrator asks: "Could God be trying to tell us something?" To Kramer, the humanist, the answer is yes: a truly compassionate moral spirit knows what the religious right will not acknowledge—God is as present in confrontations and the grappling of one lonely, struggling soul with another in the dark pines of Fire Island as He is in the most immaculate megachurch, if not more so. Kramer insists that we look at our whole human family—in the baths, in the alleys, in the board-rooms—and see God there. I know he says he doesn't believe in God, but he writes as if he does.

I said I see him as a writer in a well-established tradition. I mean the nineteenth-century novelists' tradition, when certain activist novelists used their skills—skills that Kramer uses, too—to draw our emotions into a great contemporary struggle. The novels of George Eliot about anti-Semitism come to mind, as do the novels of Charlotte Brontë about the struggles of workers for enfranchisement. Dickens, especially, is Kramer's literary father in some ways. Dickens used our fierce concern about lovable, flawed characters to draw us deeper into feeling injustice; think of the child poverty in *Oliver Twist,* the corruption of the establishment in *Bleak House.* Dickens, like Kramer, is not afraid to wrench our emotions—or to leave a scene in a cliff-hanger. The idea that a narrative line wakes you up morally is a pre-modernist idea; "So, you're the little lady who started this great big war," as Lincoln famously remarked to Harriet Beecher Stowe. Kramer is in that tradition—the gay man who started this great big war, or insisted we notice that we were, indeed, at war.

So many of his messages here, to the younger generation, are humanist messages—so old-fashioned in a callow age that we need Kramer to make them new again: honor your dead. Take responsibility for yourselves. Grow up. Your lives have meaning—don't fuck and drug them away. Isaiah's message, and that of every Old Testament prophet, was similar: look at what you are doing. You think this shit doesn't matter but it does; you are God's children (or as Kramer would say it, we are all brothers and sisters)—everything you do matters. It remains to be seen if a callow age can rise to his call.

I would like Kramer to be read as an heir to the great nineteenth-century novelists. I would like him to be read in high-school English classes in Iowa, as well as the "queer studies" seminars in the Ivy League where he is already part of the canon. Because Larry Kramer is not a "gay writer"—though he is of course also a gay writer. He is one of those who belong to all of us, who speak to all of us about our moral choices, and he uses the great literary techniques of the pre-modernist tradition to do so.

Whether we rise to his challenge is up to us. Kramer, though, is clearly already one of the greats of our era; one of those who—regardless of sexual identity—to quote from a Stephen Spender poem, leaves "the vivid air signed with their honor."

—*Naomi Wolf*

INTRODUCTION

I HAD NO DESIRE TO MAKE ANOTHER SPEECH. I have too much work remaining on my book to take off the amount of time it requires to write a good one. I have been working since 1977 on something I call *The American People*. It is now some 3,000 pages. I am a long way from being finished. Since my liver transplant in December 2001 I operate under the assumption that my days are numbered. Each day of clarity and energy is a gift I must put to my book's advantage. So when my friend from ACT UP days, Peter Staley, asked me urgently to come to lunch with someone named Dan Carlson, a founder of the HIV Forum organization, about making a speech, I was reluctant to accept. Also, the phenomenal revival of my play *The Normal Heart* at the Public Theater in New York City had just closed and I was exhausted by that entire miraculous experience. Each performance of the play, as cherished as each actor was in it, had been difficult for me. Each time I saw it I could not help but relive, replete with tears, those horrid early years of AIDS the play recalls. Yes, I was very tired.

Dan and Peter pressed me to make another speech like the one I had made that summoned ACT UP into being in March of 1987. I understood the need. Things were very bad again for gay people, gay men particularly (if they had ever been right). Only a few months before, I'd met a very impressive young man, Jeff Whitty, who had interviewed me for *Next*, a gay publication. He was surprisingly intelligent; I had not fared well with reporters from gay publications in the past, which had always treated me like an outcast. Jeff particularly surprised me by movingly registering his fears for the inchoate nature of his life and the lives of his young friends. Where were they going, this generation of his, he worried? No one seemed to know, and no one wanted to talk about it. I was very moved by Jeff and invited him to the lunch with Peter and Dan.

I had other qualms about making a speech

again. I knew what I would have to say. I've known this fact for many years. And I still didn't know if I had the guts to say it yet, out loud, in public. I well remember that when *Faggots* was published in 1978 a lot of my friends stopped being my friends because of what I'd said, crossing the street to avoid me, writing or saying asshole things about me to the media, which many still do, assailing me for what has always been labeled as my puritanical and/or self-loathing attitude. Since Day One of what has become known as AIDS I have fervently been imploring everyone to cool it. And now here I am a quarter of a century later making the same plea: to not fuck indiscriminately, to use condoms, to cool it, to make the distinction between sexual freedom (which of course I favor) and promiscuity (which is killing us). I still live in a population of people who are unable to confront the realities of the acts our bodies perform, even when these acts are true killing fields. How long can I go on making speeches that, it is more than apparent, few listen to? Is it not time to face the fact I have refused to confront since 1981: that gay people are simply never going to get anywhere as a solidified group claiming the power that would be ours if we did? Was it worth one last-ditch stand to try again? Particularly when, as I knew, this time I had to add to my previous admonitions harsher realities I had been reluctant to identify so publicly before?

Anyway, for whatever reason, I agreed to make the speech. I always wonder why I seem to be the only one around to make these kinds of angry speeches; after all the horrors of these past years, it pisses me off that there are not one hundred, one thousand gay men and women out there making them. But there never are. A few days later I backed out. I was still too exhausted. And when exhaustion occurs now—after all my body has been through—I fear my energy won't return.

A month or so later I woke up and realized that election day 2004 was near. And that John Kerry was a total wimp. And that George W. Bush was going to win big. And that the end of our gay lives was nearer than the day before. And that I felt well enough to make a speech about it.

I am always surprised when anyone shows up for anything of mine. I did not expect what confronted me at Cooper Union: a full house, with standing room, of some 900, and some 400 or more turned away. Many of them, as I hoped, were young people. I could sense their hunger for direction, just as I could sense my own—how do I name it? insufficiency? presumptuousness? inability?—in offering it. The Great Hall in Cooper Union is where ACT UP had met for years. I could feel all the dead young men haunting me who had been in this very place with me then. And on this very stage, and at this very podium, Abraham Lincoln had spoken to his people.

That Lincoln spoke here seemed some sort of omen: for the past several years I had worked very hard indeed—and against repulsive, odious opposition—to help bring to publication *The Intimate World of Abraham Lincoln*, by C. A. Tripp, the first book to present Lincoln as an active homosexual from his youth until his death. It was, at long last, coming out in barely two months' time.

This experience of fighting to get this revolutionary book about our most revered president out into the world had dramatized for me yet again what I have long believed and what my book, *The American People,* is about: nobody wants to know when the most important history of all involves people's sex lives. Because Abraham Lincoln and George Washington (to name but two) were gay, the history of our country was changed. But try to get that taught in the schools. Try to get gay anything taught in the schools.

As if to clear my head, I received an e-mail from Virginia Apuzzo, an old friend and a great gay leader and activist from earlier days: "I feel that we have a moral obligation to create havoc, to generate outrage, to reignite our belief in our capacity to do whatever your ACT UP kids did, 'change history.'" Could this be possible again? Could the young people of today experience that feeling of being completely engaged, of running a hundred miles an hour? We'd felt like we could change the world and we did.

There are a few remarks I would like to make about this speech now that I have given it. There is little in it about lesbians. Since HIV originally captured mostly gay male lives, it has been to us that I have directed most of my writing. Lesbians were wonderful helpmates in the early days but then fell away from the battle. I often wonder why they have been so silent about the gay male behavior that has, let's face it, usurped most of the gay political agenda since 1981. You would think a few of the women would have had the courage to speak out against this usurpation, to demand quite rightly that some attention be paid to the many issues that are theirs. And that perhaps their brothers might stop behaving so selfishly as to wipe them off the map. But, for the most part, they have not. Lesbians are as invisible as they have always been. That is a harsh statement to make but I stand by it. The women have been spared my criticism long enough. They are as desperately needed in the fight for our survival as the masses of invisible gay men are.

I think you should know a few things about the history of this plague that I didn't include in my too long speech.

The AIDS plague was allowed to happen because of the behavior of three men, two of whom I can call gay: Edward I. Koch, the mayor of New York from 1978 to 1989, and Dr. Richard Krause, from 1975 to 1984 the head of NIAID, the National Institute of Allergies and Infectious Disease, part of the National Institutes of Health. The third is Ron Reagan, Jr., son of the former president of the United States.

Let me leave Junior until last. Koch, of course, many of us had known was gay. For one thing, the late Judge Richard Failla, a Koch appointment to the bench and a gay man I had put on the Gay Men's Health Crisis board of directors, had confirmed it to me confidentially years ago. In 1984, I was approached in Los Angeles by Richard Nathan, someone a few of us had heard about but had been unable to locate. He told me what we had been told, that he had been Koch's lover and was willing to go public; and that the fear of being outed had completely prevented Koch from doing anything for the epidemic erupting so quickly in his city. By the time Nathan showed up at my apartment in New York to make the public announcement he had promised me and Rodger McFarlane, then executive director of GMHC, someone had got to him and, by his own admission, he had been silenced. We could not talk him out of it. He said he was frightened, which was obvious to Rodger and me, and he indicated that he had been exiled to California in the first place and he had to go back there. He had thought he might be able to rise above it and he sadly apologized that he could not. He immediately returned to California, not to be heard from again until his death from AIDS and, ironically, the establishment by his will of a foundation to help closeted gay people deal with their homo-sexuality.

For those of us involved in activism then, we knew how worthless all the window dressing being trumpeted by Koch as "doing something" was: the endless meetings in various headless and gutless departments, for instance, and an absolutely despicably out-to-lunch health commissioner, Dr. David Sencer, who positively shook when confronted with what his department was not doing. To this day Koch maintains his heterosexuality and how much he did for gay people. Rodger and I and others have by now combed the records and we defy Koch to produce concrete information/evidence of what the fuck he or his administration actually did to help us deal with AIDS. We can't locate a thing. Of all the people in the world I condemn Koch as the person most responsible for allowing HIV to grow unimpeded from forty-one cases to the more than 70 million now being tallied. It was on his watch it all began. He could have sounded the first and most important alarm; to the city, to the president, to the media, to the world. In any and every way he did not do so.

The case of Dr. Richard Krause is a more perplexing one. Why didn't he do anything? I have been told by those who worked for him that nothing was done during his years as NIAID's director. His associates knew he was gay and he knew they knew. He was a worldwide expert on infectious diseases and had written widely about them. There is no way he could not have known what was happening. After all, it is NIAID that would have been and still is responsible for any possible scenario of response and action. Evidently he just chose to wait and see. He has been quoted to me as saying, in effect, much the same: it's only a few cases now, let's wait and see if they go away. He refused any cooperation, partnership, or input from the Centers for Disease Control, an agency he evidently had animosity toward, which was the only government entity that was involved in doing anything to track what was going on. How he continued to maintain a "wait and see" attitude in the face of the quickly mounting case numbers the CDC was tallying is one of those questions he should be asked when he is on the stand at a Nuremberg-type trial that will of course never be held. How could he have behaved like this? Was Richard Krause ordered by the White House to lay off? After all, Gary Bauer, who hates gays like I hate snakes, was Reagan's domestic policy adviser and was calling many shots. In 1983 I'd had lunch with Krause in his house on the NIH campus. He produced all kinds of reports both of us knew were bullshit. He then left me there with his assistant who turned out to be gay. I went to the only bathroom, upstairs across from Krause's bedroom. An industrious reporter investigates all available avenues. His bureau top was covered with framed photos of handsome men, most of them in bathing suits. The assistant confirmed my suspicions: the son of a bitch was gay. The top man in charge of the most important government agency that could have done something to sound the alarm of this plague that was no longer coming—it was here—and commence attempting to identify it was out to lunch. Like Koch, it was on his watch it all began.

I detail in my speech what happened during these first four years: that because no one was doing anything to stop it, to warn the world, to urge caution, the virus took hold without opposition pretty much all over the world. Lacking even the most timid of warnings, gay men during this period were thrilled to carry on their death-defying behavior unimpeded.

Nothing was to change until Dr. Anthony Fauci replaced Dr. Krause as head of NIAID. Another thing that becomes more and more obvious to me as I continue to review again and again what was and was not done during these earliest years is this: that after a very rocky few years while he got started (I certainly came after him with all my might), Dr. Fauci has become and remains the one and only true AIDS hero in our entire government. Whatever is being done, and while it is now too late to save most of the world's presently infected, it is now substantial and it is all being done in some part because of Dr. Fauci. He remains sadly a lonely hero in that vast behemoth that is not only the NIH but also the USA.

I cannot say that I know for a fact that Junior is gay as I know that Koch and Krause are. But the rumors persist and I have been privy to many of them, some more detailed than others. When his father was running for president in 1980 on the very eve of our plague, it was no secret that many thought Junior was gay. This popular belief, coupled with his image as a ballet dancer, must have been on the mind of his father and his mother and their many political advisers. It must have been on the mind of many on the Christian right, a crucial constituency for his father. It must have been on the mind of every Republican who desperately wanted his father to win. Next thing, Junior is appearing with Doria, an older woman his mother did not even like. Then off with the tutu (or whatever male dancers wear) and on with the wedding ring. The two remain married. This has never stopped the rumors. There is no question in my mind that because of Junior Mr. and Mrs. Gipper refused to allow any talk about AIDS because that would mean talking about gays and that would mean even more rumors about Junior.

One wonders what it must be like to have lived in Junior's skin all these years. What was it like for Junior—who apparently had many gay friends from prep school, from Yale, from the ballet, from life— to stand by silently while his father condemned them to death?

Then, too, his mother. Her many gay friends, how did she look them in the eye? What incredible hypocrites the entire family are! The father in his younger days slept around in Hollywood. So did his mother. Ronnie was sleeping with another woman at the very time he was about to marry Nancy.

And Nancy reportedly had her own "best friend" when she attended the all-female Smith College; she was also exposed to a major lesbian network of her mother's best friends. Nancy's own "social" life before and after her marriage remains the talk of Hollywood. Who were these people to cast down such severe judgments of the lives that anyone leads?

This was our First Family during those hideous first seven years of AIDS. There is no historian who can dredge up any excuse to account for their wretched, ghastly, inhumane, immoral behavior toward gay people and toward what was already a plague. Or to write about it! No one writes about this. No one writes that Ronald Reagan has been responsible for more deaths than Adolf Hitler. If a president wants to do something, he does it. George W. Bush took us into war! Ronald Reagan did not want to do anything about AIDS! Stop making excuses for him. Stop ignoring it. He would not even utter the word AIDS in public for seven years. It was on Ronald Reagan's watch that AIDS happened.

Yes, it continues to be incomprehensible to me how all of this remains not written about, the behavior of all these people I have discussed above.

After you have finished this book I want you to reread the following paragraphs:

Sometimes a writer must work all the way through a book before he realizes what it is that he is really writing about. More and more I feel that gays shall never get anywhere as a people. More and more I feel that this is what is happening to us. There are too many of us and we have been here long enough to show us what we are made of. We have not journeyed anywhere near where we must be. Oh I know there are many reasons why. I just don't buy them or accept them anymore.

I desperately wish to be proved wrong. Come, any and all of you, I beg you. Please prove me wrong!

Sometimes the challenge makes the man. Unlikely heroes arise. It is up to you whether you choose to be heroic or not. The fight is never easy. But it must be won.

—*Larry Kramer*

THE TRAGEDY
OF TODAY'S GAYS

(A speech made at New York City's Cooper Union on November 7, 2004, five days following the reelection of President George W. Bush, presented by the HIV Forum in conjunction with New York University's Office of Lesbian, Gay, Bisexual, and Transgender Student Services, Broadway Cares/Equity Fights AIDS, Callen-Lorde Community Health Center, and the Gill Foundation)

I THINK THIS HAS BEEN THE MOST DIFFICULT speech I have ever had to write and to deliver. It is a long speech. I pray you will bear with me until its end.

It is an attempt to give you some idea of who and what we are up against. It is also an attempt to discuss our ability to deal with these.

I recently learned about two dear friends, both exceptionally smart and talented and each in his own way a leader of our community. One, in his middle age, has seroconverted—that is, he has become HIV positive. The other, in his middle age, has become addicted to crystal meth. Both of them are here with us tonight.

I love being gay. I love gay people. I think we're better than other people. I really do. I think we're smarter and more talented and more aware. I do, I do, I totally do. And I think we're more tuned in to what's happening, tuned in to the moment, tuned in to our emotions, and other people's emotions, and we're better friends. I really do think all these things.

To us it defies rational analysis that Bush, this incompetent dishonest man, and his party should be reelected. Or does it?

I hope we all realize that, as of November 2, 2004, gay rights in our country are officially dead. And that from here on we are going to be led even closer to the guillotine. This past week almost 60 million of our so-called fellow Americans voted against us. Indeed 23 percent of self-identified gay people voted against us, too. That one I can't figure.

The absoluteness of what has happened is terrifying. On the gay marriage initiatives alone: 2.6 million against us in Michigan, 3.2 million in Ohio, 1.1 million in Oklahoma, 2.2 million in Georgia, 1.2 million in Kentucky—George Bush won his presidency of our country by selling our futures. Almost 60 million people whom we live and work with every day think we are immoral. "Moral values" was at the top of many lists of why people supported George W. Bush. Not Iraq. Not the economy. Not terrorism. "Moral values." In case you need a translation that means us. It is hard to stand up to so much hate. Which of course is just the way they want it.

Please know that a huge portion of the population of the United States hates us.

I don't mean dislike. I mean hate. You may not choose to call it hate, but I do. Not only because they refuse us certain marital rights but because they have also elected a congress that is overflowing with men and women who refuse us just about every other right to exist as well. "Moral values" is really a misnomer; it means just the reverse. It means they think we are immoral. And that we're dangerous and contaminated and dirty. How do you like being called immoral by some 60 million people? How do you like being thought of as dirty? This is not just anti-gay. This is what Doug Ireland, the fearless gay journalist, calls "homo hate" on the grandest scale. How do we stand up to 60 million people who have found a voice and a president who declares he has a mandate to do their bidding and not ours?

The new Supreme Court, due any moment now, will erase us from the slate of everything possible in no time at all. Gay marriage? Forget it. Gay anything good, forget it. Civil rights for gays? Equal protection for gays? Adoption rights? The only thing we are going to get from now on is years of increasing and escalating hate. Surely you must know this. Laws and regulations that now protect us will be repealed and rewritten. Please know all this. With the arrival of this second term of these hateful people we come even closer to our extinction. We should have seen it coming. We are all smart people. How could we not have been prepared?

They have not exactly been making a secret of their hate. This last campaign has seen examples of daily hate on TV and in the media that I do not believe the world has witnessed since Nazi Germany. I have been reading *Ambassador Dodd's Diary;* William E. Dodd was Roosevelt's ambassador to Germany in the '30s, and people are always popping in and out of his office proclaiming the most awful things out loud about Jews. It has been like that.

All Mary Cheney is is a lesbian! Even her mother is hateful! That Cheney must be one fucked-up kid to stick around that family. I hope she doesn't want to teach school. A newly elected United States senator vows to make it illegal for lesbians to teach school.

I know many people look to me for answers. Perhaps that is why many of you are here. You want answers? We're living in pigshit and it's up to each one of us to figure out how to get out of it. You must know that by now. Crystal meth is not an answer. You must know that by now. And quite frankly, statistically it is only happening to so few of us that it is hard to get anyone worked up about that problem. Just as it is hard to get worked up about a middle-aged man with brains who seroconverts. You want to kill yourself? Go kill yourself. I'm sorry. It takes hard work to behave like an adult. It takes discipline. You want it to be simple. It isn't simple. Yes, it is. Grow up. Behave responsibly. Fight for your rights. Take care of yourself and each other. These are the answers. It takes courage to live. Are you living? Not so I can see it. Gay people are all but invisible to me now. I wish you weren't. But you are. And I look real hard.

No one likes to be told to grow up. It's insulting. But these are always the answers. They will always be the answers. The only answers. There will never be any other answers. Grow up. Behave responsibly. Fight for your rights. Take care of yourself and each other. Be proud of yourself. Be proud you are gay. I don't know why so many find all this so complicated. But then, I am sixty-nine years old and have less patience for the many problems I had myself when young. It is one of the privileges of getting old.

It is twenty-five years since 100,000 of us marched on Washington.

The AIDS service organizations are all about to collapse. No money. And the problem is too big to handle anymore. We have not slowed this thing down at all. One hundred billion dollars we're spending on Iraq. This is a conscious choice by our "leaders" and by a large portion of the population of this country. They have in their infinite and never-ending cruelty decided this was the most effective thing to do with $100 billion that might also end AIDS, and a few other things like worldwide hunger. But the cabal doesn't care about these. People say: well, we can't take care of the rest of the world. That is so stupid. The rest of the world is us. We are so intertwined geopolitically that we cannot separate ourselves off into parts, into sections. Those days are over. If they ever were here. We have everything required to save the world except the will to do it. In a recent *New Yorker* article Michael Specter writes that because of AIDS, Russia is on its way to disappearing. Disappearing. Imagine that.

The immense knowledge we have learned about AIDS has provided us with precious little more than that knowledge. HIV/AIDS is now the worst disaster in recorded human history. In parts of Africa, 7,000 people are infecting one another each and every day. We who are here are idiots if we think this fact is not going to alter our lives mightily. If your company loses enough world markets, which it most certainly will, you are going to lose your job. You will not have health insurance, for a start. And for a finish. Economies are simply going to collapse. This is already happening.

In 1990, that is some nine years into what was happening, 46 percent of gay men in San Francisco were still fucking without condoms.

Sixty percent of the syphilis in America today is in gay men. Excuse me, men who have sex with men.

Palm Springs has the highest number of syphilis cases in California. Palm Springs?

I do not want to hear each week how many more of you are becoming hooked on meth.

HIV infections are up as much as 40 percent.

You cannot continue to allow yourselves and each other to act and live like this!

**ONE OF THESE DAYS THE MIRACU-
LOUS DRUGS WE HAVE TO KEEP US
ALIVE ARE GOING TO STOP WORKING.**
Our systems cannot process these extreme
chemotherapies indefinitely. That is what we are
on. We are on daily chemotherapy. No one wants
to call it that. We call it the cocktail. We are on
chemotherapy! Chemotherapy either kills the disease or kills us! What are we going to do when
these drugs don't work any longer?

Some 70 million people so far are expected to
die. "July 3, 1981, rare cancer seen in 41 homosex-
uals." When I first started yelling about whatever it
was, there were forty-one cases. **There are now
more than 70 million who have been infected with
HIV.** Somebody up there is really listening, don't
you think? **There is no way that all infected people
can be saved.** No one ever says that **OUT LOUD.**
Have you noticed? Somehow in some dream world
we were going to get treatment into 70 million people. **It is never going to happen! It is too late.** We
told them. **But they didn't do anything.** Did you

notice? Nobody ever does anything. I hope it's finally dawning on you that maybe they didn't and don't want to do anything. So, in case you haven't noticed, we have lost the war against AIDS. I thought I'd tell you that, too. I hope you might have noticed. I can't tell.

WE HAVE LOST THE WAR AGAINST AIDS.

George W. Bush has refused to buy generic drugs for dying people. He dawdles by saying he is waiting to hear if they are safe. Many of these generics have been approved for a number of years. In some cases, for a number of years. And when they haven't been safe, they have quickly been made safe. Does this sound like a president who wants to save anyone?

I do not understand why some of you believe that because we have drugs that deal with the virus more or less effectively that it is worth the gamble to have unprotected sex. These drugs are not easy to take. There are many side effects. Not necessarily life-threatening yet, but certainly comfort-

threatening. I must allow at least one day out of every few weeks to feel really shitty, to have no sleep, to be constipated, to have diarrhea, to require blood tests and monitoring at hospitals or in doctors' offices, and to have the shakes. The shakes are not useful when using a mouse or reading a newspaper or holding a lover in your arms. I have dry mouth. I get up six or seven times a night to pee. Many of the meds we are now taking are new meds and were approved quickly and side effects have a sneaky way of showing up after FDA approval, not before. I recently discovered that I was taking an FDA-approved dose of Viread that has turned out to be five times the amount I actually need. We are all probably taking too much or too little of every single one of our drugs. Doctors don't want to test for this; tests are not readily available. You have to do a lot of homework yourselves on these drugs. Is a fuck without a condom worth not being able to enjoy food? Obviously for too many of you it is.

My lover, David Webster, has had to sit on top of me to make me eat. I don't enjoy eating anymore.

Keeping on weight is a constant problem. The first time this happened I was in the hospital just after my liver transplant and I wouldn't eat and Dr. John Fung, who had just saved my life, said I had to eat, or else I would die, and I just couldn't eat (do you know how strange this is to someone who was always on a diet?). It was New Year's Eve. We were in beautiful downtown Pittsburgh. David had brought a hamper filled with my favorite dishes. And I could not eat anything. Furiously he crawled into bed with me, boots and all, and started to cry. "We haven't come this far for you to die because you won't eat," he screamed, tears streaming down his face. I will never forget that. I will never forget this man I love so much in bed with me with his snowy boots on starting slowly to spoon into me whatever he'd made and I trying so desperately hard to swallow it, looking at him, this man I love so much, doing this for me, both of us now bawling our eyes out and hugging each other in this strange bed in this strange town, wondering how we got here.

It's so wonderful being a gay person. I said that

before. I'm going to say it again. I love being gay. And I love gay people. I think we're better than other people. I really do. I think we're smarter and more talented and more aware. I do, I do, I totally do. And I think we're more tuned in to what's happening, tuned in to the moment, tuned in to our emotions, and other people's emotions, and we're better friends. I really do think all of these things. And I try not to forget them.

Since the very first day of this plague we have been given, almost as if by some cosmic intentionality, American leaders who most assuredly wish us dead. There can no longer be any way to deny this fact. Each day brings more and more acts of hatred against us. Tell me it is not so. Tell me that the amount of good that is being attempted is not totally and intentionally overwhelmed by the evil. Point out to me how this is not so. I cannot see it. I have been unable to see it since July 3, 1981. I thought it was because it was a tricky virus. That is what we had been told. It's a very tricky virus. I hoped for a while. But we are being played for chumps and it has been so since July 3, 1981. And we never saw it.

We of course continue to be in our usual state of total denial and disarray. Whatever structure the gay world had, if we ever had one, is gone. Our organizations stink. Almost every one of them. Despite the best will in the world, most of them are worthless to us. Oh, maybe the legal ones are good. We have no power. Nobody listens to us. We have no access to power. The cabal disdains us totally. We are completely disposable. It is a horror show. There is not one single person in Washington who will get us or give us anything but shit and more shit. I'm sorry. This is where we are now. Nowhere. And you expect me to cry for you if you get hooked on meth or can't stop the circuit parties or the orgies. Okay, I feel sorry for you. Does that change anything? I would say I feel sorry for myself, but I don't. I know I am fighting as hard as I can. I may not be getting anywhere but I am trying. It's exhausting and I have to do it every day, every single day, like taking my meds which, if I stop, I know my body will cease doing something or other. I have accidentally missed a few days of meds and, boy, do I know fast that was a mistake.

I fear for us as a people. Is that crazy? I am always being called crazy by somebody. I love being called crazy. That's a sign to me that I'm on the right track. Maybe it takes a crazy person to see into the future and see what's coming. Straight people say, "My, how much progress gay people are making. Isn't that *Will and Grace* wonderful." **If it's so wonderful why am I scared to death?** If it's so wonderful why are 60 million people voting against us? More and more I am filled with dread. That is my truth that I bring to you today. Larry is scared. Do you see what I see? I don't think so. Most gay people I see appear to me to act as if they're bored to death. Too much time on your hands, my mother would say. Hell, if you have time to get hooked on crystal and do your endless rounds of sex-seeking, you have too much time on your hands. Ah, you say, aren't we to have a little fun? Can't I get stoned and have the thrill of fucking without a condom one last time. ARE YOU OUT OF YOUR FUCKING MIND! At this moment in our history, no, you cannot. Anyway, we had your fun and look what it got us into. And it is still getting us into. You kids want to die? Because that's what I sometimes think. Well, then, die.

You cannot continue to allow yourselves and one another to act and live like this!

And by the way, when are you going to realize that for the rest of your lives, probably for the rest of life on earth, you are never going to be able to have sex with another person without a condom! Never! Every time you even so much as consider this, I want you to hear my voice screaming like crazy in your ears. **STOP! DON'T! NEVER! NO WAY, JOSÉ!** Canadian scientists now warn that even partners who are both uninfected should practice safe sex. As I understand it, more and more new viruses and mutant viruses and partial viruses that are not understood are floating around. Are you ready for that one?

Does it ever occur to you how much you have

been robbed by both your country and your behavior? America let the men who should have carved out a space for you in the social discourse, the development of your history and being, America let these men who should have been your role models die. So there is this big empty space in which you live. And you don't know where to go or how to fill it in. This is not my original thought but Michael Brown's of the NYU gay student organizations that helped to bring me here, who gave me this to think about. It is sad for a young gay person to feel this way.

I had people to follow and many of you have not. No baton was passed to you. In a way you must start everything over. You must invent a world from which you can move forward. This is both an extraordinarily exciting challenge and a terrifying one, one that can just as easily leave you by the wayside as make a new man of you. I say man because it is gay men who appear to have the greatest difficulty, it seems to me, in moving forward, getting off their particular dime.

Many of you deny the horrors of what happened to your predecessors. That is something I do not understand. Every moral code I know of requires respect for the dead. I often hear that many of you don't want to know about them or admit to them. You disdain anyone older who was there.

This is denial of a most destructive nature. You cannot move forward without accepting your past. I am going to say that again. We cannot move forward without accepting and understanding our past. We were as varied as you are. We were no different, really. We were very different from those who preceded us. We were the first free gay generation, and we were murdered because of our freedom. And, yes, you were robbed of this freedom that for obvious reasons could not be passed on to you as your heritage. So, instead of being understanding of all this, you condemn your predecessors to nonexistence and flounder into a future that you seem unable to fashion into anything you can hold on to that gives you emotional sustenance. You refuse to be part of any community. But if you don't have any community, you have no political strength. You are too busy denying and disassociating to know that. You do not seem able, it seems to me, to fashion your future. To discover what you want. You don't even ask what you want. You don't even ask what you need. Your needs are as mighty as needs always have been, but you don't ask what they are, which amazes me. How can you not have curiosity about your future as a gay person? Don't you want to go anywhere? Do you want to stay where you are? That is too bad if you do because we are about to enter a place more monstrously worse. You can deny that, as you deny those of us who went before you, but just know that down this path of your numerous denials lies your own continued destruction, the continuing destruction of gay people as gay people, which this cabal of haters I shall shortly describe, and its supporters, who are legion, are intent on accomplishing with increasingly ruthless vengeance. If you do not fight back, you will be murdered in ways just as hideous as the ways in which we got murdered.

Every single president since 1981 has denied our existence and denied the existence of AIDS. And we let them get away with it. Oh, a few thousand of us fought for the drugs that we got, but many millions of us did nothing and of course an enormous number of us died. They died because they lost their health along their journey of noninvolvement and their lack of responsibility to their brothers and sisters. Instead of learning from this lesson, you are repeating it. And you are acting like this with your health intact, many of you, which strikes me as even more perverse than what your dead predecessors did to destroy themselves.

Does it occur to you that we brought this plague of AIDS upon ourselves? I know I am getting into dangerous waters here but it is time. With the cabal breathing even more murderously down our backs, it is time. And you are still doing it. You are still murdering each other. Please stop with all the generalizations and avoidance tactics gays have used since the beginning to ditch this responsibility for this fact. From the very first moment we were told in 1981 that the suspected cause might be a virus, gay men have refused to accept our responsibility for choosing not to listen, and, starting in 1984, when we were told it definitely was a virus, this behavior turned murderous. Make whatever excuses you can to carry on living in your state of denial but this is the fact of the matter. I wish we could understand and take some responsibility for the fact that for some thirty years those fucking without condoms have been murdering each other with great facility and that down deep inside of us we knew what we were doing. Don't tell me you have never had sex without thinking down deep that there was more involved in what you were doing than just maintaining a hard-on.

I have recently gone through my diaries of the worst of our plague years. I saw day after day a notation of another friend's death. I listed all the ones I'd slept with. There were a couple hundred. Was it my sperm that killed them, that did the trick? It is no longer possible for me to avoid this question of myself. Have you ever wondered how many men you killed? I know I murdered some of them. I just know. You know how you sometimes know things? I know. Several hundred over a bunch of years, six or seven or eight years, all the while mumbling to myself "the law of averages is still on my side," I have to have murdered some of them, planting the original seed. I have put this to several doctors. Mostly they refuse to discuss it, even if they are gay. Most doctors do not like to discuss sex or what we do or did. (I still have not heard a consensus on the true dangers of oral sex, for instance.) They play blind. God knows what they must be thinking when they examine us. Particularly if they aren't gay. One doctor answered me, "It takes two to tango so you cannot take the responsibility alone." But, you know, in some cases it isn't so easy to answer so flippantly. The sweet young boy who didn't know anything and was in awe of me. I was the first man who fucked him. I think I murdered him. The old boyfriend who did not want to go to bed with me and I made him. The man I let fuck me because I was trying to make my then boyfriend, now lover, jealous. I know, by the way, that that guy who was fucking me is the one who infected me. You know how you sometime know things? I know he infected me. I tried to murder myself on that one.

Has it never, ever, occurred to you that not using a condom is tantamount to murder? I cannot believe you have never considered this. It is such a simple and intelligent thought to have. And we all should have had it from Day One. Why didn't we? That has been haunting me for a long time, that question. Why didn't we? It is incredibly selfish not to have at least thought that question at all those moments when we were playing Russian roulette.

From here on, I am going to get more complicated. I want you to pay attention. This is the most important part of this speech.

Bill Moyers recently said this in a speech on October 20, 2004, at New York's Palace Hotel: "For years now, the corporate, political, and religious right—this is documented from 1971 on—the religious and political right has been joined in an axis of influence whose purpose is to take back the gains of the democratic renewal in the twentieth century and restore America to a rule of the elites that maintain their privilege and their power at the expense of everyone else. For years now, a small fraction of American households has been garnering an extreme concentration of wealth and income while large corporations and financial institutions have obtained unprecedented levels of economic and political power over daily life.

"Take note," Moyers continues. "The corporate, political, and religious conservatives are achieving a vast transformation of America that only they understand because they are its advocates, its architects, and its beneficiaries. In creating the greatest inequality in America since 1929, they have saddled our nation, our states, and our cities and counties with structural defects that will last until our children's children are ready for retirement, and they are systematically stripping government of all its functions, except rewarding the rich and waging war."

In other words, our country has been taken away from us by a cabal that includes all the people who hate us.

These people make the rules. They are rarely elected officials. They may or may not know one another personally, but they manage to stay in constant touch. They have several things in common. They are very rich or have strong connections to money or power. They are in agreement on what they do not want. They believe fervently in their God. And that they are doing everything for Him.

I hope you realize that all these people Bill Moyers is talking about hate us. Thriller writers write better histories of our times than actual historians.

Anyway, it is done. What Moyers is talking about. It's already happened. On a scale of such magnitude that it is difficult to see how we can ever take it back. It's all in place now, this cabal of power. It almost doesn't make any difference who is president.

You want to know why AIDS was allowed to

happen? This is your answer. You want to know why gay people have no power and are unlikely to get any? This is your answer.

The top 1 percent of wealth holders control 39 percent of total household wealth.

The richest 5 percent of households own two-thirds of the value of all stock owned in our country.

The top 1 percent have as many after-tax dollars to spend as the bottom 100 million.

The richest 20 percent of households received almost 50 percent of the national income, while the bottom 20 percent received only 3 percent.

At a time when 265 people in the United States were billionaires, 32 million people were living below the official poverty line.

This inequality gap in the United States is the highest in the industrialized world.

"That drive," Moyers continues, "is succeeding with drastic consequences for an equitable access to public resources, the lifeblood of any democracy. From land, water, and natural resources, to media and the broadcast and digital spectrums, to scientific discovery and medical breakthroughs, and even to politics itself, a broad range of American democracy is undergoing a powerful shift in the direction of private control.

"We are experiencing a fanatical drive to dismantle the political institutions, the legal and statutory canons, and the intellectual and cultural frameworks that have shaped public responsibility for social harms arising from the excesses of private power."

In 1971, Lewis Powell, a Richmond lawyer who called himself a centrist, was secretly commissioned by the U.S. Chamber of Commerce to write a confidential plan on how to take back America for the survival of the free enterprise system. Not democracy. Free enterprise. Barry Goldwater had lost, Nixon was about to implode, Vietnam had sucked the nation's soul dry, the cabal saw their world unraveling. They saw the women's movement, black civil rights, student war protests, the cold war. They saw the world as they knew it coming to an end.

(We are not the first to feel our world crumbling and becoming powerless.)

This is what Lewis Powell wrote: "Strength lies in organization, in careful long-range planning, in consistency of action over an indefinite period of years, in the scale of financing only available through joint effort and in the political power available only through united action."

This was the birth of what is now called the vast right wing conspiracy. It is known as the Powell Manifesto. You can Google Lewis Powell (not the one who helped to assassinate Lincoln) and read it in its entirety.

Under the supervision of some of the richest families in America, that plan has been followed faithfully since 1971 and it has resulted in these past years of horror and the reelection of George W. Bush. Nine families and their foundations, all under the insistent goading of Joseph Coors, have financed much of this. The Bradley Foundation. The Smith Richardson Foundation. Four Scaife Family Foundations, The John M. Olin Foundation. The

Castle Rock (or Coors) Foundation. Three Koch Family Foundations. The Earhart Foundation. The JM Foundation. The Philip M. McKenna Foundation. From 1985 to 2001 alone they contributed $650 million to this conservative message campaign. They have helped to launch and gain financing for networks of newspapers and magazines. They have seen to it that hundreds of the most powerful think tanks have appeared, including the Heritage Foundation, Hoover Institute, American Enterprise Institute, Cato Institute, Manhattan Institute, Hudson Institute, and many more. There are now in place an ever-growing number of well-funded student organizations at many colleges. There are legal advocacy foundations, such as the Center for Individual Rights and Judicial Watch. There are Leadership Institutes and Action Institutes and Institutes on Religion and Public Policy and Religion and Democracy. There is a heavily visible media participation: Fox Television and Pat Robertson and Oliver North and Radio America and the *Washington Times* and Ann Coulter and

Rush Limbaugh, to name but a very few, including the editorial page of *The Wall Street Journal.*

For the preparation of this manifesto, Lewis Powell was rewarded by Richard Nixon with a seat on the Supreme Court, where among other things he voted against gays in *Bowers v. Hardwick,* and against black people in *Bakke v. University of California.*

It is vital for us to realize that this plan was written in 1971. The people it was written for did not go off then to a disco, or to Fire Island Pines or South Beach, or into therapy, or into drugs. They took this plan and they have executed it religiously every day and night for the past thirty-five years, initially with some $400 million, and always, from then until now, with unending hours of backbreaking, grinding, unglamorous work, of civic engagements county by county across the entire expanse of America. They took the richest and most liberal nation in the history of civilization and turned it hard right into a classist, racist, homophobic, imperial army of pirates. Thirty percent of America now self-identifies as conservative or extremely conservative. When Lewis Powell wrote his Manifesto, that figure was less than 10 percent.

And on the morning of November 3rd we wrung our hands and wondered why.

And we have a community that still cannot decide on what we want or what to do. We are completely inept at organizing ourselves and we have a monstrously bad record of even attempting unity.

The continuing existence of HIV is essential for the functioning of the totalitarianism under which gay people now live. It works out like this: HIV allows "them" to sell us as sick. And that kills off our usefulness, both in our own minds—their thinking we are sick—and in the eyes of the world everyone thinking we are sick. All of this obliterates the consciousness of those who should help us and don't. This liquidates and incinerates our individuality and our spontaneity, our abilities to fight back, to hold our oppressors to task. **THEY WANT TO KEEP HIV GOING AS LONG AS**

THEY CAN! Why haven't we seen that? The signs have always been there! But like everything else, we couldn't believe them. No one could be as cruel as that. They want to make us superfluous. Their media, their newspapers, their networks will see to it that our good qualities are invisible.

It should therefore come as no surprise that when HIV came along they, this cabal, facilitated its rapid deployment and continue to do so. Before even making the feeblest attempt to commence any minuscule response or inquiry into what their press was not reporting, which they most certainly knew about themselves, they waited until masses of us had all been exposed to the whatever it was. We, on the other hand, chose to not believe that the whatever it was was a virus until this was incontestably proved. But they knew what it was, or were willing to take the chance and hope that it was, and they just sat back and waited. Their wildest dreams then started to come true. The faggots were disappearing and they were doing it to themselves!

I can locate no work of any urgency, or indeed

much work at all, on AIDS, for most of the period between 1981 and 1984. Oh, many claim it, as many claim seeing cases many years earlier, which I also doubt, but I cannot locate it. In those four years almost every gay man who had fucked without a condom in America had been exposed to the possibility of infection by the HIV virus.

And when they did start doing anything, it was with such feebleness that it amounted to nothing for ten years. You can give me all kinds of reasons why it took so long but my research has convinced me that the actual scenario was one of completely intentional neglect. Oh, perhaps not the doctors or the scientists. But they had no money. And they were not going to get any money. Or enough money. People upstairs were going to see to it that there would be no money. Let even more people get infected first. Blacks, junkies, prostitutes. Every color of skin but straight white. Every religion but Christian. Excuse me, white Christian. Then we'll throw them a few pennies to make it look like we're concerned.

The cabals Bill Moyers talked about have called all the shots in facilitating and accelerating the plague of AIDS. If scientists discovered something useful, it has rarely been readily available. I spoke earlier about the refusal of this president to allow already approved generic drugs out to a desperate Africa and elsewhere. Of that huge congressional approval of many billions for HIV around the world that Bush brags about, something less than 2 percent has actually left Washington some four years after its approval. Does this sound like a president and a government and a country that want to help?

I guess I have suspected behavior like this all along. But I never knew it in quite the way that I have now come to see it thanks to Bill Moyers: intentionality is the only word to describe the genocidal treatment millions of bodies have been drowning in. Much of the world, most assuredly including us, has been intentionally hung out to die. So far some 70 million of us. That is some manifesto Lewis Powell birthed. And all we have to do is keep fucking each other without condoms and the rest of their "moral issues" will be dead.

Do you seriously think they care about the continuing rise again of HIV infections? They are grateful for them. Do you think they care about a sudden plague of crystal? They thank us for our cooperation. And we thought for one brief second of time that we might even be allowed to marry the ones we love.

And while all this happened, even if we had enough suspicions to act, what did we do? We completely shrank from our duty of opposition. Those are Christopher Isherwood's words: "the duty of opposition." But he was flagellating himself with these words. He feared, faced with a war in his backyard, he "would shrink from the duty of opposition."

Marriage? Forget it. Nondiscrimination laws? Forget them. Those that have been enacted will be rescinded or amended into toothlessness. Adoption? Equal rights? Forget everything. We are going to be erased into nothingness. They hate us so much and now they are in complete and utter power, the most dangerous situation in the world for the unwanteds to live under. And I no longer think it matters who is president. Clinton turned out to be as rotten for us as George Bush, both of them, father and son.

Okay, keep putting your life in jeopardy—110 of their drug companies certainly want you to do so. Keep dancing your asses off at circuit parties all over the world as you go down to the sea in ships that are made to intentionally capsize and take you down with them. Okay, keep being bored and crying for your poor selves. You ain't seen nothin' yet. With our complete cooperation they have already murdered several generations of us so far. They won't have to murder so many more of us to get their wish. Like Russia, we will disappear. That is what they want to do. Disappear us. And now they are able to officially do it. George W. Bush has his mandate. Can't you see all this! People high up there in their secret powwows don't want us here. Word has come down from on high: get rid of the

faggots once and for all. You think the law will protect us? Think again. Wait until you see any new
Supreme Court.

You are here as a gay person because of certain
events and certain people who lived and suffered
and died before you. You must learn about them
and not continually deny their existence and importance in our history, the history of gay people
in America. You must learn about them! They
have made your life possible! What kind of people
don't want to learn about themselves? I don't
know why but you don't. Most of our fellow gays
don't read books about us. Or come to plays about
us. What do you want to do? I don't know. And
for all I can tell in talking to many of you, you
don't know either. And this is very frightening. A
large uncongealed mass of potentially superior beings doesn't know what to do with itself or bother
to learn its history. So they dance. So they drug. So
they go on the Internet to find more sex. These are
useful lives being wasted. Why is that? Why is
there no useful creativity going on? Why is there

no mental agility visible, no audible questioning discussions about . . . almost anything of importance? Don't you long for some involvement in the humanity that you belong to, for your place in the scheme of things? You don't know how to make entrance on these playing fields, is that it? I don't know what is wrong with you. I wish you could tell me. **What do you do with yourselves all week long, seven days and nights a week, that amounts to anything really important?** I can't see many of you as doing anything important to give your lives meaning. Oh, I can see lots of frocks on the runway, but I can't see bodies inside them with brains and concerned with anything but pretty and orgasms. What do you do to make your world, our world, a better place? A world that needs every bit of help it can get, our world, not their world. You don't seem able to connect with anyone beyond the basest ways.

GET OUT THERE! DO SOMETHING FOR EACH OTHER!

"Why can't we look at our bodies and see not just a sexual definition? Why can't we see in the body all that the body represents? Sexuality, yes. But also mortality, humanness, humaneness, innocence, purity, intelligence, health, sickness, strength, consideration, responsibility, divinity. When did we rob our bodies of all the complexity they possess? Why do we refuse to see all that we are capable of? All the other things that make us full beings." That very beautiful paragraph was written by my young friend, Jordan Roth, who is one day going to be a very fine writer if he just keeps at it.

Do you know you are taking the same crystal meth as Hitler? The stuff that was being used well into 1997, the government outlawed one of its ingredients; so the original process was resurrected, the one used by the Nazis. The Germans first synthesized it in the early part of the twentieth century. Hitler was a crystal addict. The new version is much more potent than the stuff you were taking before 1997, which is the main reason why it is now so hard to break an addiction. Dr. Howard Grossman, executive director of the American Academy of HIV Medicine, told me this bit of history. Maybe I shouldn't have told you about the Hitler part. To the more twisted among you, it may be a turn-on.

I love being gay. I love gay people. I think we're better than other people. I really do. I think we're smarter and more talented and more aware. I do, I do, I totally do. I really do think all of these things. And I try very hard to remember all this.

But I am finding that I am not so proud of being gay today as I was yesterday. It's come over me slowly. As much as I love being gay and I love gay people, I'm not proud of us right now. It's slowly disappeared, this pride. It's becoming injured. I almost could say we've disappeared. But since so many of you are here, I can't quite say that. But that's how I feel right now. I don't want to. I desperately want to feel full of pride again.

I do not see us, don't you see? I do not see us! They are killing us. They are eradicating us from this earth. Little by little by little we are disappearing. I do not see us, and I am beginning to see us less and less.

I have recently come to believe that gay men and

women are tragic people. We are so wonderful but we are also so fucked up. So blind. So ignorant in ways to look after ourselves. So uninterested in the Outside World that is disappearing us when we thought we were making them pretty and giving them songs to sing. So without agendas. So without any idea how to utilize our wonderfulness. We know who the enemy is and we just stand here letting them shoot us over and over again. **We stand here and let them do it!** All of the brains and abilities we have among us seem useless. The smartest among us, our famous ones, our rich ones, seem to allow this most of all. The ones who should help us and speak up for us refuse that responsibility. We have enough rich gay men and lesbians to finance a takeover of the world but their brains and their money and their skills are not available to help us. To lead us. To inspire us. To finance us. That, too, is tragic. To have so much money and to not use it for brothers and sisters, for family, for our continuation here on earth. Why is that? Rockefeller tithed his fortune from his very first dollar, to go to his church for his salvation. Please, can we get word to every rich gay person to show up to help save us. We need all of them desperately.

Public service: how many religions demand this of their members? How much public service on behalf of your brothers and sisters, your family, have you performed recently? Don't tell me you don't know what to do. If you can find another ass to fuck, and you seem endlessly inventive at accomplishing this, then you should be able to locate a more useful and responsible outlet.

For a few brief years we had some noble moments of togetherness and progress and anger. Not many of us, mind you. If you are still alive, you know who you were and where you were during those worst years of our mass murder. You know what you did and what you didn't. And I know, too. I know that most of you, should you still be alive, didn't do a goddamned thing.

In fact, you were ashamed of us, many of you were. I remember that as well as I remember those who died. "Friends" crossing the street to avoid me because I was advising guys to cool it. I was actually told not to come back to Fire Island Pines. People come up to me now on the street and say thank you for what you do for us. I do not consider that a compliment. My response quite often has been a curt "Fuck you! Why aren't you doing it, too?" I don't do anything that anyone else can't do. I just do it, and some 10,000 other people did it then, too. And the rest of you sat on your asses. And those of you who are still alive know who you were and how little you did.

Yes, for one brief moment in time we got angry. Correction, a few of us got angry. Of all our many many millions of gay people in this country, about 10,000 of us or so got angry enough to accomplish something. We got drugs. We got AIDS care. We got enough so we could continue fucking again. That in the end is what it amounted to. As soon as we got the drugs, you went right back to what got us into such trouble in the first place. What is wrong with us? The cabal can't believe their good fortune.

How many gay people were in America in those early years of AIDS? Twenty million? Thirty million? How many of us are there now? We don't even know how many of us there are! Or how many we lost! And every time some statistical number is released by some faceless government organization I always wonder, How the fuck do they know how many of us there are when we don't even know how many of us we are? And none of our so-called gay organizations ever bothers to find out. It would be nice to know, helpful to know. Don't you think?

You know, it isn't meant to be easy, life. I don't know why it isn't meant to be easy but it just isn't so we might as well get used to it and try to find things that give us a certain sense of pride. We must create ourselves as something we can live with. It takes energy, yes. Why are we so crippled intellectually? Oh, we study sexuality and gender stuff until it comes out of every university's asshole but we don't study history, our history, who we were and where we came from and our roots, the wellsprings of our historical existence. We do not honor our dead as we do not honor ourselves. We continue without surcease to be and remain, endlessly, day after day, helpless victims. "In my country when they raise the bus fares, we burn the buses," a Brazilian journalist said to me as she watched a sparsely attended ACT UP demonstration.

There is never one single hour that a disenfranchised minority does not have to fight to breathe and stay alive. The hate out there will never lessen. It only grows and grows, this hate. Most of you refuse to face this. Or to even admit that it is hate. I have no more patience for this kind of weakness and blindness. I know this is uncharitable of me. But I am so very, very tired of fighting with so few troops. You are now dancing your own dance of death, you know. Grow up, I beg you. Oh, grow up.

Time goes by so fast. We are allotted so precious little of it on this earth. How sad when we use it so stupidly. Every second that goes by is gone forever.

You who have been given a new lease on life, the very gift of life itself, piss it away. It is so incomprehensible to me who has come so close to death a couple of times. I find your inactivity and ingratitude and lack of imagination on how to act in, or even to recognize, emergencies incongruous, incomprehensible, insulting. And unacceptable. I could never understand during all those years of AIDS why every single person facing death would not fight to save his own life. And I cannot understand now how, life having been given back to us again, again you treat your life with such contempt.

Yes, all that I have spoken of tonight is the stuff of tragedy.

I wish we could truly look upon each other as brothers and sisters. I am told it sounds corny when I keep using a term like this. How can we be related? I am asked dismissively. You do not know or want to know that we have been on this earth as long as anyone else and that we have as many available heroes and heroines as any other group of people.

Your family, your brothers and sisters, have been here a very long time and have an ancient and distinguished lineage. You must learn that Abraham Lincoln was gay and George Washington and Meriwether Lewis and so many others we are only just beginning to uncover. But they will not let gay history be taught in schools and many universities. And we seem unable to teach ourselves. My own college, Yale, with $1 million of my own brother's money to do just this, has yet to teach what I call gay history, unencumbered with the prissy incomprehensible imprecise, fuzzy gobbledygook of gender studies and queer theory. Abraham Lincoln would not understand that kind of stuff. I do not understand that kind of stuff.

We richly deserve the government we have received. We do not even know who we are. And our enemies participate in their convictions every day of their lives. We only show up when we want to, which is not very often. But then perhaps you do not love being gay. Or think we are better than other people. And smarter. And more talented.

And more tuned in to what is happening. And are better friends.

I leave the hardest topic we must face till last.

How do we fight as a united front—for that of course is what we all must do—when they don't approve of our "behavior" and when our behavior is inseparable from our beings? How do we fight as a united front—for that of course is what we must do, or die—when some of us won't or are unable to change certain behaviors that many of us have difficulty in supporting and defending ourselves? We've been so concerned about showing the world a united front, which is quite correct. But we feel the need to say that everything gay people do is good and this simply isn't so. We must have an honest discussion amongst ourselves about what's harming us and what's helping us as a people. This is of course the problem that has finally brought us down because, from the very beginning of gay liberation itself, whenever that first really was, and I don't know when that first really was, and no one else does either, we have refused to deal with it (and perhaps this is one reason today's youngsters have difficulty in acknowledging our past). It is this un-faced devil in our closet, if you will, which, now, now that they have achieved such imperial power, will be used to hang us once and for all. To be crude about it, how do we market and sell our wishes and our needs and all our selves as they have been able to package and sell all their wants and needs and selves so successfully for thirty-five years? How do we frame this issue of our many sexual practices? It is inhuman to think that the only way we can get through to some safe other side is by policing each other and in so doing destroy whatever hope we have of getting along.

And how do we claim the God that they have gobbled up for their own private reserve? If they have been able to convince this country that the Republicans are the party of the people, surely so many sons and daughters can be smart enough to find a way to sell our own parents on the idea of permission to coexist, one nation, under their same God.

I do not know how to answer any of this. And I

don't think anyone among us does either. To talk out loud about what our bodies have done and continue to do is asking for trouble. How do we admit our past, and for some of us still our present, and own it, and evolve from it and move on? For we must do this. If, for one reason alone, to keep ourselves alive. We cannot afford to lose many more of us along the wayside.

I know some of you will immediately jump up to act. I caution rushing off to form anything quite so fast until we decide how we want to deal with what I have raised tonight. I know many of you are prepared to tough it out and say to them, "Fuck you, I am what I am." And point out quite rightly that they have simply pushed us too far and, no matter what we have done and continue to do, we simply cannot allow them to treat us this way any longer. We are human beings as much as they are, and their God is the same as everyone else's God and He simply cannot be allowed to be as punishing as they are requiring Him to be.

But this is perhaps too honest and rational to say to those who are not either about us. Reasoning like this has not worked for us in the past. But I sense that ignoring this question of responsibility for much that has murdered us will only pleasure them more.

These are the problems we must confront as we go forward. If you are going to fight in a united way, which I hope you are convinced is the only way that can save us, we must find a platform that all of us can support without divisiveness and shame and guilt and all the other hateful weapons they will club us with.

And if we do want to go out and fight again in a united way—and I pray we will—we must ask ourselves: are we able to replicate the kind of devotion and commitment and backbreaking, thankless work and tactics that continue to bring them year after year into such positions of unlimited power? Thirty-five years of that? For thirty-five years the cabal I have spoken of has worked every single day and night to bring them their many successes. Quite frankly, they deserve their victory as, so far, we deserve our loss.

I would like to quote this from a heterosexual minister, Tom Ehrich, who lives in Durham, North Carolina. By chance, a friend, Jane-Howard Hammerstein, found it on a Christian Web site this very afternoon. "It would be helpful if we started in silence and just listened to each other's voices. Whether we can muster such maturity amid toxic political attitudes remains to be seen. If we are to have a meaningful national discussion of moral issues, we will need to start with the sexual issues, not because they are the most important but because they are the fire engulfing the tower. Let's get it all on the table. . . .

"And let's do so openly and boldly, without the code language that we often use in moral debates, without our usual cherry-picking of Scriptures, without our usual blistering indignation, without the bullying that elevates one's viewpoint into divine certainty."

So we are being invited to this table whether we want to be or not. We must be prepared.

I love being gay. I love gay people. I think we're better than other people. I really do. I think we're smarter and more talented and better friends. I do, I do, I totally do. I really do think all of these things.

And I passionately and desperately want all my brothers and sisters to stay alive and well and on this earth.

Brothers and sisters, can we all help each other reach this goal?

AFTERWORD
BY RODGER McFARLANE

"YOU'RE A BUNCH OF FUCKING SISSIES!"
That's how I first remember Larry spitting mad at
a group of us for whatever we weren't doing fast
enough or big enough or courageously enough. It
was the summer of 1981 in the Greenwich Village
apartment of Paul Popham, a corporate executive
and former Green Beret—who with Larry and four
others was a cofounder of Gay Men's Health Crisis. I don't recall specifically why Larry was casti-
gating us that particular evening—pick an issue.
AIDS had just been noticed by the medical establishment and media. No one was doing anything
about it; Larry thought we should. Paul, who would
become president of GMHC, was closeted, so no
one but Larry would speak to the press—and then
Larry would be screamed at for whatever he said.
It's not the merits of Larry's arguments that evening
that stuck with me. Twenty-four years later, I just remember marveling at his manifest belief that we
could accomplish anything that we decided to—

and that we were shit if we didn't. That he was calling a room full of grown men, many of them self-made millionaires, cowards to their faces—and that they were taking it—just earned him bonus points with me. I was smitten on the spot and ready to follow the guy with the big mouth and brass balls anywhere.

I wasn't just civically inspired. Soon after that, Larry and I started dating and eventually lived together a while. That social footnote is only important for those knee-jerk critics who since *Faggots* and throughout the plague have accused Larry of being sex phobic.

To them I say, "I know something you don't." Early in the crisis, Larry *had* said we all should "cool it" until we knew what was going on. He never said, "Stop fucking," although that's what most gay liberationists inferred and is why many excoriated him and continue to do so. In 1981, 1982, and 1983 many of us were still epically drugging and screwing our brains out, and there was a good chance, we all suspected, that something contagious was getting passed around. Larry was the only one saying so publicly at the time, so he made for an easy target.

Another favorite diversion from any critical examination of our sex lives and the morality of our sex lives was and still is dismissing whatever Larry said as hysterical or hyperbolic. Larry certainly made abundant use of drama and hyperbole in his activist speeches and in his political writing—but the accuracy of his charges we didn't have to debate as long as critics could speculate on his motives instead of the implications of what he was saying. It's worth recording, too, that in time Larry's direst predictions—dismissed as deliberately alarmist in the early '80s—came true.

Larry's singular voice drove the creation of hundreds of AIDS service organizations across the country, leveraging hundreds of millions of dollars a year and fielding tens of thousands of volunteers, creating the only safety net at the time and even now—all the while amassing a huge body of clinical expertise and moral authority unprecedented among any group of patients and advocates in medical history. Even more significant, what Larry published and what he wrote and said to individuals in high places, and what he said relentlessly and loudly to the public through every media outlet from *New York Native* to *Nightline,* led directly to the first of many congressional hearings on the federal response to AIDS, and the first state and federal appropriations for AIDS monitoring, services, treatment, and research. All this initiated seminal reports from the Office of Management and Budget, the Surgeon General, the National Academy of Sciences, the Institute of Medicine, and others—documents that to this day define the AIDS dialectic at the highest levels.

ACT UP was born in 1987 when Larry substituted at the last minute for director/writer Nora Ephron in a lecture series at the Lesbian and Gay Community Services Center in New York City. His speech called on all of us in the audience to start ACT UP, that night—us, right then. I best recall the heyday of ACT UP as endless weeks of tedious collective meetings punctuated by spectacular public demonstrations with hundreds of smart, hot men and women flashing ultraslick graphics, chanting pithy slogans, and getting hauled away. (If you don't grasp that democracy and good citizenship entail draping Jesse Helms's house in a giant condom or chaining oneself to a pharmaceutical executive's desk or shutting down Wall Street at rush hour, then, as Larry would say, you don't know history.)

But that was just the on-camera action. Directly under Larry's tutelage (and, yes, nightly harangues), some of us nouveau activists schooled ourselves rigorously in the minutiae of medicine and pharmacology and statistics and in the arcane procedures and economics of government and corporate science. Larry and his comrades married savvy public pressure with masterful media manipulation, naked coercion, occasional litigation, and adept behind-the-scenes political and corporate maneuvering that led directly to sweeping institutional changes with vast ramifications.

Among the concrete achievements that grew out

of that one last-minute speech in 1987: accelerated approval of investigational new drugs; expanded, compassionate use of experimental drugs and new applications of existing drugs; mathematical alternatives to the deadly double-blind-placebo-controlled studies of old; rigorous statistical methods for community-based research models; accelerated and expanded research in basic immunology, virology, and pharmacology; public exposure of and procedural remedies to sweetheart practices between the National Institutes of Health and Food and Drug Administration on one hand and pharmaceutical companies on the other; institutionalized consumer oversight and political scrutiny of FDA approvals for all drug classes and for vast NIH appropriations for research in every disease; state drug assistance programs; and vastly expanded consumer oversight of insurance and Medicare and Medicaid reimbursement formularies. Each of these reforms profoundly benefits the health and survival of hundreds of millions of people far, far beyond AIDS and will do so for generations to come.

And the drugs themselves! We must never forget that just about all treatments for HIV/AIDS being used today around the world are out there because in some way ACT UP and its sister organizations like Project Inform in San Francisco got them there.

Larry's greatest civic legacy, to my thinking, is permanently dismantling the old system, once and for all wresting control from the pharmaceutical companies and government scientists, and placing treatment decisions for all conditions directly into the hands of patients and their doctors. He also, along the way, cultivated a generation of exceptional activists and writers.

Shortly after Larry agreed to give the speech you see in this book, he despaired and called me. I encouraged him to tell us all why he was hopeless, and why that enraged him (and me) and broke his heart (and mine) and how it boggles the (our) mind(s) that folk so good and smart and beautiful could throw away their lives instead of finding great purpose in them, and how ultimately, bitterly tragic it all is. I also sent Larry a copy of a secret memo Lewis Powell wrote in August 1971, two months before Powell was nominated to become a justice of the Supreme Court, outlining a plan to ensure the dominance of free enterprise in perpetuity.

I had taken a new job in 2004, running Tim Gill's foundation, the largest focused on winning lesbian, gay, bisexual, and transgender equality. (Tim is also the most generous gay political contributor in America.) When Larry called about the speech, we at the Gill Foundation had just spent several months earnestly trying to figure out how to jump-start the gay rights movement, after years of legal gains followed by brutal setbacks at the ballot box. Our network of leaders and organizations was scattered, fragile, and universally undercapitalized. We'd been playing life-and-death defense in Washington for years, while at the same time getting our asses relentlessly kicked state by state. Compounding it all, our opponents had ten times more money and a thirty-year head start.

That's why Justice Powell's now obscure manifesto was on my desk and on my mind when Larry wondered aloud what he was supposed to tell people to do. A veteran Democratic operative named Rob Stein had shown me Powell's work last year. Rob was as deeply concerned with the disarray of the other progressive movements as we were with the LGBT movement. He'd been studying the religious fundamentalists and political conservatives, trying to figure out why they're so effective and why we're not. I was a preprimed audience for Rob because I'd just digested a research report called "Axis of Ideology," prepared and published by the National Committee for Responsive Philanthropy, which tracked the hundreds of millions in annual donations from the handful of superwealthy Americans bankrolling basically everything conservative: their think tanks, policy institutes, leadership development programs, university centers, media watchdogs, judicial watches; vast publications and giant media networks; their direct connections and lavish fund-raising for the Republican leadership; their close ties with parallel ultraconservative religious and quasi-religious organizations like Focus on the Family and their constituent networks; their direct funding and board oversight of many of these same groups; their alliance with and funding of parallel issue-based movements like antiabortionists and gun lobbies; and their deep relationships with multiple lobbies for giant multinational industries.

What we have not learned from our opponents—what we glimpsed momentarily at the height of ACT UP but failed to institutionalize then—is not so mysterious. What Larry calls on each of us to do, and has all along, is nothing abstract. It's actually quite grinding and unglamorous and takes decades of stamina and discipline to pay off. If we don't act now and act effectively, we're going backward another fifty years politically and legally, and hundreds of thousands more of us, incidentally, again will die unnecessarily along the way. We've got no coherent strategy, across leaders or groups or funders. We have feeble grass-roots muscle; we can't turn out votes or campaign contributions sufficient to win almost anything, anywhere, ever. Right now there's not enough money in the LGBT movement (or the AIDS movement) to come anywhere near competing with or advocating effectively against our well-organized, well-funded adversaries and the sheer scope of our challenges. A big hunk of the money that is available isn't spent particularly wisely or even tactically. And most of our richest and smartest gay folk aren't doing a fraction of what they should and must. Nor are many millions of rank-and-file gay Americans doing half as much as those millions more on the other side who are writing checks sacrificially, constantly educating and organizing their families and their coworkers and their neighborhoods, actively informing themselves, and sounding off and voting en masse on every conceivable issue in towns and counties across the country.

Ultimately, though, we've all, including Larry, failed to capture the hearts and minds of other

Americans. Our opponents pander directly to fear, hatred, and bigotry, painting us as a threat to the nation and to stable families. We respond with legalistic demands. We have failed to appeal persuasively to the values, emotions, and beliefs of most mainstream voters, and there aren't enough of us to fight for our lives, much less our equality, without the compassion of straight Americans—or at least a bit less of their bile.

For those of us in a position to do so, this means we have to bring a great deal more money to the fight if we want a serious crack at prevailing. We also need a practical plan that gets us off the defensive and focused on serial wins. It means that we need our very own proper think tanks and solid research, evidence on which to base winning strategies and messages beyond our firmly held opinions and political maxims of the past. We need our own well-trained, well-paid managers running our own thriving advocacy groups and building us a future in every state. We also need street activists and legal armies and corporate heroes generating the social capital and political will to succeed long term. We have to pass laws and defeat laws. We have to elect candidates and defeat candidates. When we lose, we must make it painful and expensive to have taken us on. We desperately need ruthless lobbyists in Washington, and we need to roundly expose our would-be elected and appointed enemies before they ever get to the statehouse or on the bench. Gay people and those who love us must embrace full-contact political engagement pretty much everywhere. And we have to sustain it, likely forever. That's how the other side did it and holds on to it.

There remain two things that cause my hope to waver. Some of our brightest still choose to get high and fuck blindly instead of passionately seeking great purpose for their precious lives. I, like Larry, do not and probably never will understand why gay people either proceed blithely along with business as usual, or actively destroy themselves instead of fighting back. It's the saddest thing I've ever seen, mainly because I've watched it play out so often and for so long.

What continues to concern me more is the apparent inability or refusal of thinking folk to recognize that many Americans hate us, hate us to death. They are in fact repelled by us and specifically by what makes us different. Last spring many of us thrilled at the image of Phyllis Lyon and Del Martin, pioneering activists and devoted companions for more than fifty years, marrying in the San Francisco City Hall. Even the most jaded operatives like me welled up with pride. How could any fair-minded citizen deny these two old patriots their measly Social Security benefits? But float that picture of Del and Phyllis kissing among a focus group of college-educated women under fifty—those Americans who allegedly make up our most promising allies—and half the room giggles nervously or says yuck, while two have to excuse themselves altogether. Researchers refer to it as the "ick" factor, but it's far more sinister than that sounds. No matter how cleverly we package our so-called issues and our very selves, there's no avoiding the pervasive and carefully cultivated association that gay still means gay sex to most people and that revolts them.

At the end of an earlier version of his speech, Larry had written, "One hopes." I asked if he honestly did have hope for our future. He told me he'd been rethinking that line for this book. I don't believe he's included it.

—*Rodger McFarlane*

ABOUT THE AUTHORS

Beginning in 1981, Larry Kramer has been a writer and activist fighting against the AIDS plague and on behalf of gay rights. He was a founder of both Gay Men's Health Crisis and ACT UP. Among his works are the Oscar-nominated screenplay for D. H. Lawrence's *Women in Love;* the novel *Faggots;* a collection of writings on AIDS, *Reports from the holocaust;* and *The Normal Heart,* which was named one of the 100 Greatest Plays of the Twentieth Century by the Royal National Theatre of Great Britain. Since 1978, he has been writing *The American People,* a very long book about his country. He is HIV-positive and the recipient of a liver transplant and an Award in Literature from the American Academy of Arts and Letters. Kramer graduated from Yale University, where his brother, Arthur, has established the Larry Kramer Initiative for Lesbian and Gay Studies.

NAOMI WOLF's books include *The Beauty Myth* and *The Treehouse: Eccentric Wisdom from My Father on How to Live, Love, and See.* She is a cofounder of the Woodhull Institute for Ethical Leadership.

RODGER MCFARLANE is executive director of the Gill Foundation, and former executive director of Broadway Cares/Equity Fights AIDS and of Gay Men's Health Crisis. Rodger is the author of *The Complete Bedside Companion: No-Nonsense Advice on Caring for the Seriously Ill* and was coproducer of the original commercial run of *The Destiny of Me.*